AFTER THIS, NO MORE COMPROMISING

"THIS" IS A PROCESS

Trenee Douglas

Order this book online at www.trafford.com
or email orders@trafford.com

Most Trafford titles are also available at major online book retailers.

Printed in the United States of America.

ISBN: 978-1-4269-7190-7 (sc)
ISBN: 978-1-4269-7191-4 (e)

Trafford rev. 10/07/2011

 www.trafford.com

North America & international
toll-free: 1 888 232 4444 (USA & Canada)
phone: 250 383 6864 ♦ fax: 812 355 4082

DEDICATION

After This, NO MORE Compromising is dedicated to YOU the reader! My motivation behind telling my experiences is to prayerfully be transparent enough that you will become infected and affected; by the powerful strength and hope that can be found on the pages of this book. I strongly believe that our life experiences are not only to help shape us and develop us into being better people, but more importantly; our experiences should be beneficial for others. How can I truly help someone without telling them where I've been? This question speaks very loud and extremely clear. This is not a book for entertainment, but you should search its pages for opportunities to be blessed. In every spoken or written word, life or death can be found. Through this book, please search for life! Be Blessed!

I DEDICATE THIS TO YOU, MALE and FEMALE!

Table of Contents

Introduction

<u>"No Clue"</u>

"COMPROMISE NOT," are the words that have been shut up in me since February 6, 2005. This two word message that appears to be so small and minute in comparison to others; was and is again; like fire shut up in my bones! It's an urgency that I have in my spirit to not compromise and to share with others the revelation that God gave me through my experiences. From February until maybe about the second week of November, I stood on this word. I wouldn't budge a little bit if I did not think that God was telling me to. This caused trouble in my social life. Folks misunderstood me. They didn't understand that I didn't want to be just another churchgoer, but I wanted to truly exemplify Christ. Something happened that shifted my focus though and I began to lower my standard. I became weary in my well doing and I BEGAN to uncomfortably

COMPROMISE. I had just started attending college again for the second time, deciding to start over as a freshman. This was a hard thing for me because I should have been preparing for graduation soon. However, that was not the case. I had to start over.

Flash back with me for a minute please. When I first attended college it was immediately after high school; 2002. I was eighteen years old telling myself that I knew who I was and where I was going. I thought everything was lovely. I had no real worries; not yet; not outside of me still being in love with my first love. Reality had not sat in. There I was an eighteen year old freshman in college. I was pretty, smart and in pretty good shape because I had been a basketball player since the age of six. Again, I thought I knew who I was and where I was going. I'm telling you, that was the furthest thing from the truth. I had a low self-esteem for as long as I can remember, but on the outside you would not have known it. I wasn't your average person that had a low self-esteem. I was not the one that wasn't going to laugh, talk or dance. I wasn't going to be shut up in a shell somewhere because I did not feel good about me, but I mingled. I interacted with everyone. I faced the part of me that I was insecure about on the inside behind closed doors. Sometimes, it was done silently and sometimes out loud through my actions. I messed up terribly in my academics and things had begun to get really bad. I was walking around with issues. I mean, I was bothered and the people closest to me didn't even know. They were not even aware of the things that I was battling in my mind and in my heart. It was then that the truth was made real to me. I had no clue as to who I was, and the opinions of the people confused me even more. So there I was, sitting in the college classrooms; there in presence, but absent in mind and spirit. I was going back and forth through my mind wondering, WHO AM I REALLY? I DID NOT have a terrible childhood. I had one of the best mothers that God created. I never had a consistent father figure, but growing up it really didn't bother me. It wasn't until around this time, that I felt the effects of not having a consistent positive male figure in my life. I have an older brother, but he wasn't always the best example before me. See, we grew up in the projects and unfortunately, my brother became a victim to our surroundings. Good dude, but made a lot of bad decisions.

I wish that I knew then, what I know right now; that God created us all for a purpose, with a purpose. Growing up, there were three of us; my brother, my sister and me. We like countless others didn't walk around with this knowledge. Knowing that we were created for so much more than what we were seeing and hearing could have made the difference. I know that if I would have known that I was created a queen before even becoming a female in the physical form and that God was going to prepare for me a king who would find me,

I would have probably waited before looking. I would have waited because according to the word of God, my husband is going to find me and not the other way around.

I know that if my brother knew earlier in his life, while growing up in the projects, that God created him in his image and likeness and gave him power and authority and dominion over all the earth, he would have never thought about calling himself God, but he might have taken pleasure in knowing that he was a god. He just was not the all-powerful God. See my brother at this point in his life chose to be affiliated with this religious group called the five presenters. The name reflects the belief that ten percent of the people of the world know the truth of existence and those elites opt to keep eighty five percent of the world in ignorance and under their controlling thumb. The remaining percentage is those who know the truth and are determined to enlighten the rest and they are the five percent nation. This is what he considered to be the truth, but maybe if he knew that God said he would make his name great and that he would supply every need, my brother would not have been walking around the city building up his reputation; so that his street name might be known. He probably would not have hustled so needs could be met. If he knew the truth about his purpose, then maybe, just maybe he would have chosen another path. Maybe we all would have! What's my point? I say all of this for one specific reason; there are many people; young and old, that do not know that they are created with a purpose. If they do know, they don't know what the purpose is. Therefore, nine times out of ten we are compromising. Compromise not, these two words that have been shut up in me for six years is about to be birthed out in the following chapters.

As you read this story about a girl on a journey to become a woman made whole, you will find her in a pattern of relationships, where she conveniently compromises, believing that her compromising will land her great rewards, but instead each time she pays a great price with her life being altered. There were four different guys, an uncountable amount of bad decisions, one woman, and her freedom that awaits her at the end. This book is designed to empower, to encourage, to motivate and to convince someone to break loose from the chains of compromise that steals from us every time we compromise what God doesn't want us to.

(Http://en.wikipedia.org/wiki/The_Nation_of_Gods_and_Earths)

NOTE: IF AT ANY POINT WHILE READING THIS BOOK, IT FEELS LIKE YOU ARE IN A CHAOTIC PLACE IN YOUR MIND, BECAUSE THE STORY APPEARS TO HAVE YOU ALL OVER THE PLACE- ITS BECAUSE THAT'S EXACTLY WHERE I WAS IN THESE MOMENTS. ALL OVER THE PLACE!!

Chapter 1

"Compromising a Gift"

It all started when I was six years old. I was the only female on an all-boys basketball team in the city of Paterson, NJ. My aunt encouraged me to play basketball. Whatever the reason was and I don't know; she did! Basketball was one of the things that helped shape me growing up. It was one of the things that I believe was used as an instrument to keep me away from a lot of the no good things that I could have become a part of. From the ages of 6-10, I played with the boys earning a respect that wasn't easy to come by as a female. Playing with boys was where I learned that there was no room to play like a girl, but I had to play like a ball player; aggressive, hard, passionate, unafraid and without any consciousness of how my hair looked by the middle of the game. It didn't matter how wet I became from sweating or how much contact that had to be made at times. It just did not matter. I was there to ball! I went to sleep thinking about basketball and I woke up thinking about it. Basketball was my life as a young girl growing up. From the ages of 10-13, I switched over to a females league and found my place there. Again, in my mind, there was no such thing as play like a girl or boy. I WAS A BALL PLAYER! Playing for Tee-M-up was an experience all by itself. I was so aggressive. I was short, stocky, and AGGRESSIVE! The referees, the coaches, even some of the parents thought I was too old to be playing in the league, but I wasn't. I had just been trained by boys. My experiences in the boy's league and the many unorganized street games that I was a part of in the projects was tough and I got some of that toughness in my blood.

There I was, in one of the first games of the season dribbling the ball back and forth between my hands. My opponent was defending me. I dribbled the ball in between my legs and then it happened. Coach snatched me out the game and chewed me out. "You are not a boy!" "If you ever do that again, you'll be on the bench." That was the beginning of my potential becoming stagnated. **"YOU ARE NOT A BOY."** Wow! So there I was walking around with this mental struggle, afraid to be me. I was afraid to play to my full potential because now my perception or idea of what a ball player was; boy or girl, IT DID NOT MATTER; a ball player is a ball player was now tainted by one of my teachers in life. (The coach) I played with restrictions from this moment on. Beginning stages of me compromising in my life started here. I changed who I was on the court and what I could do because somebody else said that it should be done. (Never change who you are and what you can do because someone else said you shouldn't be doing it. If God gifted you to do it, DO IT. - if not YOU LOSE)

June 19, 1998, graduation day is here! I'll be a freshman in high school in about three months. I'm going to Paterson Catholic Regional High school and he's going to Passaic County technical Institute, which is also a high school. Guy 1 going to Kennedy High School was not an option if our relationship was going to work and be uninterrupted by foolishness. At least that's what I thought. I was a freshman, playing point guard on the varsity team! Predictions were made of my soon to be greatness in the newspapers. Expectations were high. I was a part of a five woman crew of freshmen that were all predicted to make some type of noise on the court. I was there, but I didn't show up. I was in love! I played basketball and so did he, but here is where the issue came into play. There was no time for "us" anymore. So, I came up with the idea of quitting. Yes, this will fix our little problem. I'll quit basketball. The goal was to free up some time.

I had so many excuses that I gave the people; from the coaches, down to my mother. Excuses like, "I don't like the way the coaches talk to me." "It's too much work" and "I'm not into it anymore." but the real reason was, I quit ball because I wanted to be available to him. Now, think about this. I had been playing ball since the age of six and at this point I'm fifteen. Was I serious?! I knew a coach talking to you hard could and should come with the game. I knew the amount of work that it took to be effective on the court. I even knew that my reason for being less interested was because my focus had shifted from the gift to a boy.

This wasn't just anybody in my mind though. This was my first love, my first sexual encounter, my first time thinking; I am going to marry him! I was only fifteen years of age. Everything was going good and then he transferred from Tech to Kennedy. What I feared in the beginning about him going to Kennedy High had become my reality. Guy 1 got there and blew up! He became a big thing on the basketball team. He was popular and was truly the ladies' man. Slowly, but surely Guy 1 started to distance himself. There was little to no phone time and very little hanging out time. I was concerned. I felt troubled and needed answers.

Guy 1 did what he had to do for himself and the direction he wanted his life to move into. He told me that we needed space a part and that he was sorry, but he was not going to give up basketball and mess up his chance for anyone, not even me.

Silly me! Wow! What did I miss? I quit basketball over this boy, something that I loved doing more than anything in the world. I had great potential and ability and I gave up a possible promising future in it. It took me three and a half years to stop crying over him and about eight to stop hoping that we would reconnect. After breaking up, I went into a minor depression. I didn't want to go out, all I did was cry and regret and eat. I ate a lot. The beginning of my excessive weight gain started here and has continued throughout the years.

How often do we give up precious valuables, whatever they are, in the name of love; only to find ourselves empty left without anything except feelings of rejection, feeling unappreciated, unloved, unacknowledged, and unworthy? As if you yourself were missing something required. Noooooo! Could it be that you were just compromising the wrong things, at the wrong time, for the wrong person, for the wrong reason? I compromised. I gave up my passion for the game for him and shortly after, HE LEFT ME. I no longer had him nor did I have basketball.

Chapter 2

"Compromising a New Start"

Trying to get over and passed Guy 1, I thought maybe dating someone else would speed up the process. Guy 1 and I broke up in the year of 2000. It was sophomore year in high school and I was hurting. There was an older guy that lived up the street and around the corner, who I thought was very attractive. I would see him a lot, but I didn't take notice in him until now. He would constantly walk past the house to go to the store on the corner carrying his son on his neck, but only because I was going through this hard breakup; check for him now, was most logical. So I had an associate at the time who was next door neighbors with him tell him that I was interested. It was then that our cycle of madness began. He was a nice guy. He didn't say too much. He was kind of mysterious though. However, the mystery was not enough of a sign for me to run away. We tried dating on two different occasions between 2000 and 2002; but we just didn't seem to work during this time span. There were so many different issues present. He was an alcoholic. He was also a liar. He had several kids by two different baby mamas and on top of that; I didn't know how good of a father he was. Walking up and down the street with his son on his neck looked good, but I did not know the details of his interactions or all around involvement with his children. I didn't even know where he stood with his children mothers. He brought baby mama drama to my door steps at least two or more times. She came at me one night drunk and all, screaming how he didn't want me and how he was just with her the night before. She said so much and he denied it all, but at that same moment when I challenged him to publicly choose, he left with her. It wasn't going to work. So briefly, he and I lost direct contact. There was another older man who I ended up settling for. We had a brief relationship. He was a very nice guy also. Very respectable! He was a 30 year old African man and we saw each other for about a year. Due to his age, he wanted to get married so he claimed, but I believe there was a catch. I was not going to marry him. I wasn't trying to marry anybody at that point in my life. I was still heartbroken over Guy 1 and disappointed by Guy 2. There were quite a few things that were going on at this point in my life. I already told you, I was lost, confused, and heartbroken and I just needed a change. I needed a new start; something different. At this time; I had a best friend and I would talk to her about everything. In my mind, she was my therapist. It was the middle of 2003; we were in college and she had gotten herself in a situation that had caused us to lose touch for a while. I was left alone with no one to release to. I started drinking lightly. I was heartbroken, lonely and very confused about life itself. I was on a journey, just trying to figure life and my circumstances out. It seemed as if I couldn't. I wanted to quit. I started having pre-suicidal thoughts like; "I just wish I can end all of this." " Life is to hard God, why don't you just come and get me?" Pre-suicidal thoughts, that's what they were. Nineteen years old and I was thinking thoughts like this. I had enough sense to think to myself; if I'm thinking like this now, it's a great possibility that I'm not going to make it to see thirty. This is where I really embraced that I needed a CHANGE. I needed HOPE. I then recalled a friend telling me about her church in the past. So I decided to attend the upcoming Sunday. The church name was "The House of Purpose". It was founded by Pastors D&DE. Once I got there I found a gift, I found PURPOSE. It was one of the realest, most intriguing and attractive experiences I've had in my life. I found destiny, purpose, a calling, a loving God and an empowered word. I had to get back to that place the following Sunday, I returned to just experience the atmosphere again, but I left with so much more. I got saved and I joined the church. Everything that I knew and had become aware of that was contrary to the Word of God; I gave it all up. From cursing, to drinking, to sexing, to smoking cigarettes; I gave it up. I needed God badly and I knew it. So at this point; I'm a member at The House of Purpose and I was attending with the two females that introduced me to the church. These two women were experiencing God every Sunday. They would cry out with tears falling from their faces. They would break out into praise with a dance. They were jumping up and down. They even would speak in unknown tongues, as it appeared. All of this messed me up. I had changed my lifestyle. Again, I gave some stuff up, but I knew for a fact that some of the things that my friends were doing were most of the things that I was doing before I got saved. They were doing even more; but they were experiencing God. I was like wait a minute; I'm changing and letting some things and people go and I don't feel God anywhere on me; let alone in me. I couldn't see him or hear him or even feel him. I sacrificed what I wanted and what I knew to be comfortable; but I wasn't seeing any results for myself. This discouraged me and confused me. It even left me a little bitter at the time. So instead of hanging in there; seeking spiritual guidance and understanding, I retreated. A few months of going and then I stopped. Sure enough, Satan saw it as an opportunity to strike.

Weighed down with the feelings of abandonment, rejection, and just feeling like the value that was in me had not yet been recognized by man; I ran backwards to Guy 2; I was looking for voids to be filled. This time we kicked it off. We were together; him, me and somebody else. A few months went by and things were looking good. He came around my family and I went around his. Eventually we started having sex this time. I thought because of the amount of times we tried to deal with each other and because I had known him for a while and feelings were running high on my end; that there was great potential for our relationship. You see that? I WASN'T even SURE about how he felt on his end and I was sexually involved with him. Anyway, I told you we were finally together; me, him and yes someone else too. Three months after becoming sexually involved; something went wrong in my body. I became irritated in my private area. This discomfort was there for about a week and a half or so before I went to the doctor.

There I was in the doctor's office; in the room and the doctor asked," What can I do for you Ms. Douglas? "I began to tell him how the problem started out with an itch that became unbearable. I told him that I believed from scratching extensively that I had cut myself up and caused it to get infected. The doctor told me to get on the table and to open my legs. He then looked between my legs, walked over to the door and called for assistance. His assistance came in with some tools and the doctor warned me, "This is going to hurt, but don't move." He began to scrape off of what I thought was skin for testing purposes. He then gave his assistant whatever it was that he scraped off of me to test and then he said, "Ms. Douglas, you did not cut yourself from scratching too much. You have been infected with an STD." I went stupid. "Excuse me Doctor, a STD?" Please refresh my memory; tell me again, what is a STD? Again, I was having a little girl moment. I had lost all knowledge of old taught lessons in health class. The doctor answered and said "You've been given a sexually transmitted disease that is INCURABLE, called herpes." My heart hit my feet and I had become numb. "Oh ok doctor!" That was my response. "Thank you!" I then headed towards the door and the doctor said, "I'm sure of my diagnosis, but your results will be back in 2-3 days." I was numb, totally numb. There I was on the dollar bus, lost in my mind, feeling nothing. I got home and that numbness went into my living room with me. Wow. How did this happen? Why did it happen? I'm no loose female. I'm not sleeping around with multiple partners or anything. I'm in a monogamous relationship. There MUST be some type of explanation for this. Surely he didn't step out on me. All I wanted and needed was to hear him say, I did not cheat on you, This could have been a bold face lie, but it was what I wanted and needed. All he had to do was say it. The fact that it was lie would not have mattered. I was in denial. I didn't want to face the truth that I was not the only woman that he was sleeping with.

I called Guy 2 on the phone and asked him could he leave work early because we needed to talk. He replied, "Is everything ok?" "You're pregnant aren't you?" "Tell me over the phone," but I couldn't. I needed him in front of me when I told him this news.

About an hour passed and the doorbell rang. I opened the door and he walked in. "What's up?" "What do you have to tell me that was so important? " Numb, nervous, and confused, I placed my hand on his chest and said "Baby, you know I went to the doctor today right?" Slapping my hand off of his chest, he said; "yeah, yeah get to the point." I tried it again. "I went to the doctor; wellll, I went to the doctor and listen (placing my hands back on my chest) just tell me the truth, we can get through this together." He slapped my hands off his chest again and said "Listen, get on with it, say what you need to say or I'm leaving now and I don't want to hear it later." I continued to speak and said, "I was at the doctor today and he told me that I have herpes." "Just say you didn't cheat on me Guy 2 and you don't know anything about any herpes and we'll get through this." He reacted in such a way, that it would have made any other woman go straight crazy on him! Slapping my hands off his chest again, Guy 2 said, "I don't have nothing and I never will." WHAT? Where did I get it from, if not you? He told me that I went out there and picked it up from another guy because he didn't do it. He then proceeded to leave. I tried to stop him, but he pulled away and left. Guy 2 turned his phone off, changed his number, changed his residence and disappeared. The next time I saw him, it was about three months later by accident.

Sticking to his story, he maintained his innocence. At this point, I believe that I was out of my mind literally. I felt nasty, dirty, and used up. Who was going to want me now is what I recall thinking. My destructive behavior continued with this guy. Instead of pulling on God, family and professional help for support, I leaned on him more. Looking in the mirror and embracing me was impossible at this point in my life. In my own mind, I was running from everything outside of me, him and this disease. Once I got to his house, nothing but madness went on. Our time together had become painfully repetitive. We would fight; I mean verbally fight, sex, sleep, wakeup, I would cry and do it all over again. Think about that, he didn't have this disease, and was never going to have it, is what he said, but he was sleeping with me even more. I truly know that I was out of my mind. I was still sleeping with this man and without protection.

He continued to be him and I was lost, but I was tired of being lost to somebody who refused to take responsibility for what he had done. He didn't even care. He had no worries when it came to me or this disease. There I was in the face of the second man that basically said you are not worth me working at it. Guy 1 said "I'm not giving up basketball for anybody" and walked way. Guy 2 said "I'm not going to worry myself over you or this situation; I'm done with it." So I walked away because there was nothing else left to do. I lost focus again. I turned from God and turned to man. Now I'm paying for it with my life. He left me with something.

"Got Got"

I've been got, was stupid and blind for this dude

Sex this man without a condom, and I got something from the fool

Sad part is, dude response was like - what that got to do with me

I swear my face probably read - I can't believe,

 but he gave me something - and trust – it wasn't a gift

It wasn't a hug and a kiss and it was not bliss

but he gave me a lifelong commitment - without the ring and the kids

Without being incarcerated – I AM incarcerated

A prisoner of myself or maybe my health (and)

The outbreaks I can't take - but I'm a believer and a child of God

So you can believe me when I say- that I will not rot

Fold or ball up in a corner and plot on killing this nigga

I can never find it in me to pull a trigger - but even then

I still wouldn't win- because this disease will forever be my bad friend (but)

There is no point in crying anymore – because I'm living, I'm not dying

It's just a lesson learned - be careful who you side with

And definitely who you lie with - always listen to your first voice

Stay listening for the sirens - and when you hear or see them

DON'T ignore them - REPLY QUICK!

Chapter 3

<u>Forever is Such a Long Time</u>

Life! Wow. This condition is going to be with me for the rest of my life. How will I endure this? This is too much. Nineteen years old and I have to cope with a disease. I can remember thinking I don't deserve this. Where did I go wrong? Why am I here dealing with this BY MYSELF? I was so very lost and angry. Guy 2 and I were no longer involved at this point, but I wished that we were. I thought to myself often, this has to work; we have to be together because he infected me. This was "our" mess and we were going to make a life out of it together. I was still crazy in my mind, but the time had come when I had to face myself and the truth of the matter; which was; we were not going to be together. I was left with what he had deposited into me without him and I had to move on. I can remember thinking; this is too heavy; I can't carry this alone, but

I was alone. Nobody else had to deal with this condition, but me. I was tormented in my mind by myself. I had fears of spreading this condition to my mom and sister. Thoughts like, "Maybe I shouldn't sit on the toilet seat because maybe I'll expose them to it and they'll get it."

"I'll use separate soap because I don't want them to get it." I can remember in the beginning my sister whispering to my mother; "Ma, should I use different soap from her?" I walked in the room to let them know that I heard what was being said and I started to cry. She, my twin sister begin to cry too. We sat there and cried together. With her arms wrapped around me, she cried, "Tre, please don't cry, you're making me cry." I can honestly say that this was one of the seasons in my life where I saw that my sister really loved me. Every time I cried, she cried. It was like she herself was experiencing my pain. Anyway, I decided that I didn't want to have any secrets, so I told everyone who had a way of finding out by someone accidentally slipping up and telling. I didn't want to worry about a family member coming across a bottle of Valtrex in the medicine cabinet, so I exposed myself. I did not want to deal with any embarrassment if this secret ever came out. So I didn't allow for it to be one. Literally, I called family members informing them of this condition. Some of them were like, "Why are you telling me this?" "This is your business; you don't have to tell anyone." "You don't have to put nothing out there, I wouldn't". However, I had to. It was what I needed done.

This was the beginning of me getting acquainted with this condition. "Ok! Now what Tre?" This is what I thought to myself. I called hotlines. I educated myself on it, I spoke openly at a safe sex seminar, but I spoke out on no sex before marriage. I shared a poem and my experiences with doing things my way (sex before marriage) along with the many different negative outcomes that could potentially come into play. There was also a time when I had a heart to heart with my uncle who was living with us. I was really low, and I was sharing with him that I didn't know how I was going to live with this thing. My uncle at that time had just recently been diagnosed with colon cancer so he was struggling with his own condition. He had a colostomy bag that he had to wear and this was a hard thing for him. He worried about so many different things concerning that bag. We were very similar here when it came to how we thought. In front of people we were not going to be down, but we were alive and we would appear to be full of life and without a worry in front of you, but at night when we were alone by ourselves, was when we let go and got real about the pain and the condition. I could hear him fighting with himself and the condition; crying and beating on the walls like a baby who needed his parents to make the pain go away, but in the morning he was strong again. This same man, sat me down one day and said to me, right smack in the middle of his condition which was a deadly one; "Niece, this is nothing." "You can carry this." "Niece, if I can live with this; touching his bag, then you can live with that." Wow! This was powerful to me. My sick uncle just spoke words of life into me that shifted my thoughts. HE WAS RIGHT! I realized that if I was going to live with this disease, and I would be; because I had no choice; unless God took it away, that I could handle it, but I needed God.

I went back to church a few months later to The House of Purpose. Again, I embraced my reality by doing things and being transparent about my experiences. However, this didn't take away the confusion or the lost feeling that was so big in my heart. I was a little girl overwhelmed by life at the age of nineteen. There I was sitting back at "The House of Purpose" on the far left hand side of the church, again; lost, confused, INFECTED, AFFECTED and UNSURE, God found me right there in that state! He found me clothed in mess. I hadn't felt good, valued, or a single bit of happiness, let alone joy in my heart for about five months now, Nope! I couldn't really smile inwardly since I had been diagnosed, but God was there in my pew, in my seat, all over me. Wow! Now think about this; this was my first Sunday back. A few months prior to this, I got saved and joined "The House of Purpose", but left because I wasn't experiencing like I saw others were. Now, GOD is here and seemed like HIS showing up was all for me! My hands were lifted up, my heart was no longer heavy, tears were streaming down my face, a smile appeared and I could feel a presence embracing me.

"That's right Trenee, get yours, get yours!" "You just wanted to feel him for yourself." "You wanted to know him for yourself!" "Get yours!" I can hear Pastor D saying these words like it was yesterday and they were true. This was my moment! This was my first encounter with God and I knew that this disease was no longer going to have power over me, but I was going to use it as an outreach tool that God can use whenever he wanted to. I had to learn how to differentiate the times between when and when not to expose myself. If it's at the wrong time I can be ineffective. Everyone would not be able to handle or receive the blessings coming from my being transparent. So I grew in knowing when I should and when I shouldn't. I continued to go and grow in church, allowing the word and my experiences to mature me in my Christian walk. I grew tremendously in a three year time span. The word was in me; I had fire, passion, and I was tenacious. I was living sanctified and I had a heart for God's people. Somehow, along the way I had even become kingdom minded. It didn't matter what I did or what time of the day it was, I was thinking about my actions and decisions and how every last one of them could and would affect the kingdom. I was far from perfect, but I wanted God. Fortunately for me, God wanted me first!

I had connected with a sister who also wanted God and we fed off of each other. I challenged her and she challenged me. Our connection wasn't perfect nor was it always a smooth ride when the two of us was together, but God was in the midst. This was when I moved from being set on fire to burning with the fire of God in me. After I had my encounter, made up in my mind that I was going to give God my life, and got connected with another believer with the same mindset; walking in obedience to the word was easier to do. We had such a great hunger to see people free in Christ. Laughing to myself, I remember her and I would get out of cars and stop people on the streets just to tell them about JESUS WHO SAVES. We would sit on my porch just waiting for the opportunity to minister to somebody. Thinking about it now, she was always used for some strange reason to minister to addicts and prostitutes and I the person who appeared to be intimidating; like the aggressive, plus sized female who had the liquor bottle in her hand walking up and down the street cursing people out or the Muslim or even the young man that was in a gang boldly representing his set. We had so much zeal, but without knowledge. We soon learned.

This was a new season coming to me. Revelation about who I was in Christ and the work that he had for me to do had started to be recognized by me and confirmed by my head. I didn't grow up in church, but there I was, God wanted me. Wow! Youth leading, interceding, writing and speaking had become some of my responsibilities in the church. I also cleaned the bathroom for a little while. I soon learned that there was an evangelistic anointing and call on my life. I didn't know exactly what all this meant, but hey, I had purpose! Life made sense now!

The House of Purpose would have these women services, where the women of the church, unlicensed and all, would have to choose a woman from the bible to speak and or teach on for at least five minutes each. Well, my turn had come. I recall it like it was yesterday. I was fasting and praying trying to prepare for this day. I wanted to be prepared for this opportunity so I did a lot of reading and studying. I was prepared for the moment to speak, but what I was not prepared for was the moment that this man that I befriended; started to slowly, but surely unmask himself. Four days before my speaking assignment and an hour after leaving a powerful atmosphere of prayer for the church is when it happened. The pastors had assigned different people to be called out to pray for the different ministries in the church. My responsibility was to pray for the young people and I believe that the Lord had his way. Prayer across the board was powerful! Something wasn't right though. We had just left prayer together, now we were in my living room talking about the service and holiness and my responsibility in the church and before I knew it, I was getting up to put my underwear and pants back on. What in the world did I just do?

Chapter 4

Deceived By A Wolf: Still Compromising

I've come a long way from my past of Guy 1 and Guy 2. I've worked so hard to get here. I went through the process of getting over all of the hurts and fears of my past only to learn that I just got over them not free from them. Not getting healed and totally free from those things in my life that left me changed inwardly and outwardly only ushered me into making those same silly choices of compromise. This had really become A PATTERN UNRECOGNIZED AND UNIDENTIFIED. You see my struggle was always the same. There was nobody and I mean nobody that knew and understood all that was in me and all that I had to offer. At least that's how I felt. My value, I believe went unnoticed all my life. The men that I dealt with didn't know what kind of precious jewels and treasures were in me. My family didn't see the fullness of what was in me and friends couldn't see the friend that was in me and because of this I felt rejected.

I felt like all the love, energy, and faithfulness that I gave to so many people was never reciprocated. Why is it so easy for you to walk away from me as valuable as I am? I am a great woman, a great friend, sister, cousin, and niece. This question is still unanswered in my life.

Life was hitting hard, but I refused to allow life to kill me dead. No way! I wasn't going to just lie down; not naturally or spiritually. In other words my circumstances were not going to make me hate all of mankind. They were not going to leave me bitter. They were not going to harden my heart and make me look for the worst in people and they were not going to make me love any less, but in fact, I LOVED HARDER. Where people couldn't see that there was enough value and great intent in me; that's where I turned that thing around and decided that I wanted to see the good in people. I wanted to love them with a great love, a love without an agenda. Simply put, I searched for the value of the person and when I found it, I wanted to feed it with my love. So as you can see, my issue was being alone. My issue was being LOVED WRONG. I just didn't and still don't understand how any of us can come into GREAT VALUE, that's UNUSUAL and just easily walk away from it and easily not do right by it. Oh yes! I AM AN UNUSUAL BLESSING! I had an idea of this back then, but I know this now. The problem was; I allowed what people didn't know or ignored about me to cause a DEFECT in me.

Think about that. Situations and circumstances couldn't change the way I loved. They couldn't change the way I saw things and they couldn't change my attitude towards life or people in a negative way, but what it did do, was leave me with a crazy desire and need to be wanted, embraced, and kept by people, not God. It was a DEFECT. At this point I knew that God loved me. I knew that he wanted me, but what about the small people? What about the people who were just like me? I just wanted to be wanted and kept by a man, by a friend, by my siblings, BY SOMEONE WHO LOOKED JUST LIKE ME. I wanted to be wanted and kept by the people who should have wanted me and who should have wanted to keep me.

Often times we take our family for granted. Understand, they are granted to us, but when we allow the fact of them being biologically connected with or without our permission to permit us to not cherish these relationships, we hurt the people we are supposed to love. This reality takes from us. We treat our families a mess sometimes, but if I see your value and know your worth, not to mention you just being a person that deserves respect and love; I should be able to and desire to; protect you even from ME. I should do right by you. I should cherish you and keep you. If I really don't want to lose you; I'm not going to drive you away or allow you to just walk away. For example, my mother raised three of us by herself. She didn't hang out, didn't drink, and she didn't expose us to different men or different negative atmospheres. She never ran out on us. She never allowed us to need and didn't find a way to meet it. She never made up our minds for us concerning our father; she just did what God purposed her to do concerning us. She mothered! Value, love, effort, devotion, protection and so much more was in her. She was valuable to me! She is valuable to me! She is so valuable that I'm going to always IDENTIFY her value, EMBRACE her because of it and MAINTAIN a right relationship with her because she's worth it and she adds to me. I NEED WHAT'S IN HER TO CONTINUE TO WORK FOR ME. Our relationship is not perfect, but I know who I have and while I have the ability to do right by her I will.

I learned this early. God doesn't just call us to need him and do right by him, but he calls us to need each other and do right by each other also. So again, I just wanted to be wanted and kept by man. I WANTED SOMEONE TO SEE INTO ME ENOUGH TO EMBRACE ME ENOUGH TO NEVER LET ME GO. This isn't always easy, but when you find value in a person; you should move consciously and deliberately because that person is valuable.

(I KNOW I'M SPEAKING IN LAYERS RIGHT NOW, BUT ALL OF THE PIECES FIT).

This want and desire of mine had become dangerous for me because it helped develop this pattern of me losing myself to the wrong people. It didn't matter; it could have been a man, friend, a relative; most times I opened myself up too much.

It was an early morning and I was in the Laundromat washing a ridiculous amount of cloths. Standing there folding my cloths, this man approached me. He had on basketball shorts, a collared shirt and a fitted hat. "What church do you attend?" he asked. I looked at him and asked, "What makes you think I attend church?" "The Spirit never lies," he said. Not moved at all, I replied, "The House of Purpose." Guy 3 asked, "Who's the Pastor?" I loved telling people who my pastors were, so I proudly said, "Pastors D&DE!" He went on to say that he was familiar with them and that they had preached at his church before. I said, "Oh ok! " I continued doing what I was doing. Guy 3 asked me my name and I told him, but then he asked for my number also. At this point in my mind, I was thinking I'm not interested. I ignored the question and continued to finish my laundry. I thought that he would get that I wasn't interested and would leave me alone, but Guy 3 said "The Holy Spirit told me that you're my wife." I can remember standing there looking at this man like he was a fool from another planet. "I'm sorry I'm not trying to get involved at this point in my life." "I'm really just trying to figure a few things out about myself and God and I can't afford to be distracted, but take care!" I replied. "I'm not here to distract you, trust me!" "Can I have your number please?" he asked again. So again, I told him no. I continued to fold my clothes and he stayed nearby drinking a coffee. I was finally finished, preparing to leave and Guy 3 came again, "My God!" "The Spirit never lies." "You are my wife." At this point I'm about to leave the Laundromat with four huge bags. This man looked at me and said "You have a nice day!" Immediately, I'm thinking in my head (wait a minute) "God told you that I'm your wife, but he didn't tell you to help your wife carry all of these bags." Yeah right! It almost seem simultaneously, as I was thinking the thought, he came to me and said," Let me get them" and carried all four. He then asked again for my number. This time I told him no, but that I would take his. Look how gullible I was, because I thought a thought and he did exactly what I was thinking, I got soft at heart and lost focus. I took his number. A few days went by and I hadn't called, but I had been thinking about how strange that morning was. I found out that same morning in the Laundromat how much older he was and it bothered me. He was forty and I was twenty two and this just felt wrong to me. I asked a few older people whose opinions I valued, whether or not they thought Guy 3 was extremely too old for me. I explained to my mom and close friends that I was concerned about his age. Everyone told me the same thing, which was not to allow our age difference to be the determining factor. Guy 3 started to just pop up. He would be in some of the same public places that I would be in calling my name. Truly, this should have been a sign, but I neglected to read it. I was advised by one of my pastors to observe what he was all about. He told me to observe what his relationship with God was like. "Find out his feelings towards leadership and lastly pray with him" pastor said. "Let him hear you pray, but also allow him to pray." "Observe him, learn him." Unfortunately for me, I wasn't mindful that learning someone was a process and I hurried the whole thing. I called him that same night after getting this advice through email. Ring, Ring, Ring, he answered the phone. "Hello?" I said "Hi, how are you?" He said "Well, I'm okay." I went further telling him who I was and in return he made it known that he knew exactly who I was. I asked him; "Hey, can we get together for a cup of coffee or tea?" and he played me. "Umm No, I'm not into moving fast. I'm not like that." "I like to take things slow." I was like "Aaah, it's just a cup of coffee, what do you think I'm asking for?" He replied, "No, No I understand." "I just like to move slowly, you know?" This should have been the second warning, running me fast away from him forever, but the distance only lasted a little while.

Shortly afterwards, I began to see him in some of the same places that I was in again. He would pop up outside my gate with me having no idea as to how he knew where I lived. Still, my common sense was not working for me. I would be standing at bus stops and up he would pop, riding past on his bike. It seemed so like a sign at this time that maybe I should give him a chance. Maybe he was the one that God was sending for real. He would call and pop up like this out of nowhere and I wasn't feeling it. How can you one minute say you want to take things slow, but then do things like this? Ignoring the fact that it made no sense, one day we went out for Chinese Food so we could sit and talk, but to my surprise he didn't want to stay in the Chinese restaurant. He lived around the corner from the fast food spot and so he suggested that we go to his house. I was a little nervous about going with him there, but I went. Walking there, I noticed that he never walked beside me. He stayed a few steps ahead of me the entire time. I asked "Why are you walking ahead of me, in a rush?" He replied by saying "Oh it's nothing; it's just that a lot of my church family lives around here and I don't want them to get the wrong idea." Once again, I should have gotten it here but, I missed it.

We arrived at the house where he was renting a room. Once we were in his room; immediately I got to the questions that I was advised to ask him a few months back. I don't really recall his answers, but I do recall us praying. I prayed first and when his turn came, he was like, "Lord, she said it all. Lord, she said it all, what she said Lord. Amen." This was it, this did it for me. This man can't pray. Thinking, "He is NOT the one," I left his house knowing that I would never talk to him again. He continued to call though. In fact he called more. I always found a way not to talk though. I didn't want to be bothered. However, he was very persistent. He didn't give up. After a few months passing, he called one night. This particular night I was very sick with a bad cold. We talked for a minute about how I needed to go to the doctor to get an antibiotic or something in me, and then it happened. He said, "Trenee, I want to pray with you before you hang up." He began to pray and as he prayed he began to tell me different things about my spirit. He spoke of my gifts and my ability in the spirit. In other words, he made mention of how I had a gift of drawing people and encouraging people. He mentioned a few things that had been prophesied to me in the past. He spoke of my loving and caring heart. He said things I felt that he couldn't just know, unless God told him. This messed me up. After yearning for love, not wanting to be alone, and desiring for someone to see into me; it now seemed that maybe I was wrong about Guy 3.

"Surely, this is a man of God" is what I remember thinking. Naive me, we started hanging out. It was mostly in church services. My mom, from the very beginning said there's something about his eyes and there was, but that didn't move me. He was playing his part well. I didn't want for anything; I didn't have to spend money, nothing.

That night came, the end of Chapter 3. We went from a powerful prayer service to a sinful state. From this point on, everything changed, but specifically he changed. I recall him saying, "What did we do? Come on, get up Trenee, It was a mistake. God is forgiving, get up." I knew that God was a forgiver, but I was messed up that I had just sat there and allowed for that to go on, after God put me back together when Guy 2 left me broken apart. I was guilty. I was disappointed in myself. I didn't want this to happen again. So, I wanted to disconnect from him totally. I wanted nothing to do with him, but it wasn't going down like that. Guy 3 was not having it. I couldn't get rid of him. He showed up the next day with a Guinness stout, which is some type of Jamaican beer. He bit the cap off with his teeth and was like "I want to have more sex." What? Wait a minute, I said "Yesterday should not have happened, it was a mistake." "Yeah, but God is forgiving," is what he said. What? What did I get myself into? We didn't do anything that night, but there were many nights to come just like that one.

Slowly but surely he continued to unmask himself. "Marry me; God said you're my wife." I told him, before I marry you, God must tell me that I'm your wife. He didn't like that at all. Our verbal fights had become pretty consistent. If we weren't fighting over sex, we were fighting over me not marrying him.

One day this woman called my house phone and said that my number continued to appear on her husband's phone bill. She gave me his name and the number. After approaching him, he gave me a story that went like this, "I had proposed to her, but when I saw you, I knew I had to leave her alone." He said, "We were having problems anyway." "I wasn't in love with her." I was my own enemy at this point for real. Again, my DESIRE TO BE WANTED and the NEED FOR MY VALUE TO BE IDENTIFIED worked against me. Wow, he left someone for me. I was young and dumb, thinking I knew it all.

Guy 3 began to break me down emotionally. As the days went on he continued to uncover himself and I continued to be entangled.

Day by day it became harder to get away from him. I still don't understand why totally. At this point I had an idea of who I was in God and I thought that I knew who I was as Trenee. I stayed convicted because the sex continued. I knew what I was doing was wrong, but for whatever reason walking away from him was really hard. It wasn't like there was a reason for me to stay. He was verbally and emotionally abusive and I wasn't in love. Guy 3 tried to kill my spirit and for a little while he was succeeding. He would tell me that I was not a woman of God after every powerful service so it seemed. I would go home, call him up and tell him how I was empowered by the word. I would maybe share with him a prophecy given to me and he would in return say "You know, you are not a woman of God in my eyes." In front of people, he was the best man in the world. He was upright, decent, giving, and loving. He played his part, but when others were not around; I saw the real him. He tried to tell me that my friends and even some family members were jealous of me. He tried to turn me against my church and my leaders themselves. Guy 3 tried to move me to another state away from my family. He tried to kill my spirit and my support system. He would throw in my face often the fact that he accepted my disease and my inability to not have children. I can hear him saying the words, "Hey listen, after all I have accepted from you – nobody else would, nobody else will." Deep down in myself, I knew this was a lie, but it did hurt. The possibility of it being the truth hurt me.

I called myself ending what we had a few times. I'm telling you, he never made it easy. He would call and pretend to cry or claim for his body to be in pain because he was sick. He would show up at the house. He would bring flowers, food, and money. One night in particular, Guy 3 called and begged me to come over because again, we were not on great terms. I was on my last leg concerning us. He was like, "Come over please, I know I can fix this. I have something special in me that I need to give to you." Disgusted, I asked "Do you really think sex is going to fix this? That's the answer? That's the solution? Let's have sex?" Wow. For me, this did it. I'm done. Guy 3 was not the one. Don't get me wrong, there was a time that I thought I was in love with him and he could have probably been the one, but things happened and they revealed the truth. I realized he wasn't who he said he was and I wasn't feeling everything that I thought was. It was time to let go. So I did. Guy 3, still pursuing me, faithfully called and popped up.

It was clear he wasn't going to just leave me alone. He wanted something. He needed something. Who better to get it from than me? I was a young, vulnerable, naive, love seeking, needy, little girl. He WANTED something. He needed something and he wasn't finished trying to get it. What do you do when the very people or things that you are FINISHED with ARE NOT FINISHED WITH YOU?

Chapter 5

<u>Pregnant with Purpose-The Miracle Child</u>

"Marry me, God said you're my wife." "Marry me, I love you." "Marry Me, I need your help." "Marry me, you're going to have my baby." These were the four different extremes Guy 3 went to. He wasn't finish with me yet. In his eyes, there was still a great chance that I would say yes to being his wife. A few weeks passed and we were not together, but he still called and popped up like he always did. I was so angry at this point in my life with him. What Guy 1 and Guy 2 left me feeling was nothing compared to what Guy 3 was doing to me now.

One day he was by the house, just being him and he did or said something that just caused me to snap verbally. I said a few things to him and screamed from the top of my lungs, "Mamaaaaaa." I don't know why I called her as if she was going to come and get rid of him for the rest of my life, but I did. At that moment, my mother said "You are pregnant." Now mind you, I was told as a teenager that I could not have any children and if I wanted any, I would have to go to a fertility clinic. My mother knowing this boldly stated "You are pregnant. I don't care what you say, you're pregnant." In my mind, I was like "No, there's no way that I can be; they ran tests. I can't have children." As the days went on, there were a few different things that suggested maybe I was. Eventually, I went to a nearby pharmacy to get a pregnancy test. I can remember waiting to see the results read Not pregnant because surely I was NOT. However, when the screen stopped flashing and I looked closely to read Not pregnant, to my surprise the test read differently. "Pregnant." What? I was blown away. I can remember sitting there in the bathroom for a moment shocked. "I'm pregnant? What? This can't be true." I was hoping the test was defected, but my gut was saying that it's true, I am pregnant.

I can't have a baby by this man is what I said to myself. No way! We are not supposed to be together. We are not together. He doesn't love me. He doesn't even embrace the me that God has called me to be. I cannot have this baby; honestly were my thoughts. Family and friends reminded me of the report that was given to me years prior; I wouldn't be able to have children. "This is a blessing; you really want to get rid of your baby Tre?" I was torn between what couldn't be, but now is and how I wanted no connection with this man. Honestly speaking, if it was up to me, I would have probably made the wrong decision of getting rid of my child, but God knew more and better than me. When I went to the doctor it was around January 3rd, 2007. I found out that I was not only pregnant, but that I had been pregnant for a little more than 3 1/2 months. With him there by my side, he was excited, but I was afraid. I was 22 years old and pregnant by someone who didn't really care anything about me. I was scared. Looking back now I thank God that it was too late for me to abort my child, because God knew exactly what he was doing when he formed Nehemiah in my womb.

How could I now be pregnant, with SUCH GREAT PURPOSE after going through such hellish and purposeless situations with the man who assisted in the conception part of things? I wasn't happy then, but I'm grateful for the purpose and the life of my son.

There I was, I was a little over 3 months and being a single mother was not my heart's desire. So in spite of my ill feelings or better judgment when it came to him, I decided to give the relationship a real try again.

Things hadn't gotten any better, I was miserable. Guy 3 had given me an ultimatum. It was either I freely give him sex or when I got to the hard parts of the pregnancy, when it came to my hormones or sexual desires that he would not be there for me. He said that he was going to rededicate his life back to God if I didn't respond with a yes. This was ok I told him, because my heart really wanted to please God. I told him No, I wasn't going to freely give him sex. So he did rededicate his life to God. Nevertheless, those hard moments came, and when they did he tortured me with them. He would allow me to do different things to him and once I was finished, he would say, "I can't do this," and he would get up and leave. This continued for a little while. Eventually, he allowed it to go further, but afterwards he would play the blame game. I can still hear him saying "You tripped me up." "I'm just trying to please God and you messed me up." This too became another thing he tried to persuade me to marry him with.

Guy 3 had become so good at what he was doing that it was driving me crazy. I was beginning to hate him. "Marry Me, I need you." He asked again. "I'm not just going to marry you; we don't even agree on our lifestyles. I can't just marry you." He replied, "You are not a woman of God." "How can you be?" 'You see I need your help and you won't help me." He said, "That's not God." Guy 3 wanted security to stay in the country, he needed citizenship, but I couldn't just marry him for this reason alone nor could I marry him because I was carrying his unborn child. Common sense wouldn't allow me to, but more importantly the Spirit wouldn't allow me to. "Marry Me Trenee, we can't have this baby unmarried, we are Christians." Guy 3 then said the bible says "It's better to marry than to burn." Was he for real? Now I'm supposed to marry him because he wanted to have sex and for no other reason? No way! I wouldn't. I couldn't!

Guy 3 began to look for other ways. He went to the appropriate people explaining to them that he had a child on the way and that he needed security to remain here. Unfortunately, for him a newborn baby wasn't enough. He explained the only way he would be ok and secured to stay here was if I married him. Still I wouldn't budge. I wanted to help him, but I knew I was not his wife and we were not connected.

Guy 3 began to make discreet threats. "You better learn how to treat your man, before somebody else does it." "If you can't help me, I'll have to find somebody else to and you can't be mad." "Somebody else would love for me to pay them to do this." He said "Listen, if I have to go out there and find someone to help me, you and I can't be together because I want to be faithful to my wife." When I would hear him say this, I would be concerned. I was 23 years old, pregnant, I didn't have a dime or any financial security, not to mention I didn't want to be a single mother. As much as I felt like Guy 3 wouldn't be any good to either of us, I didn't want to raise this child alone and he knew it. Guy 3 used this knowledge and he continued to believe that he was going to get what he wanted.

Sick, I was sick and pregnant. Everything was going wrong. I was having problems at work with the supervisor and a co-worker, I was in an all-out war with Guy 3, and I was sick. My blood pressure was extremely high. I had protein found in my urine. I was diagnosed with gestational diabetes and I had preeclampsia. My body was retaining fluid and there was a hole in my baby's heart. I was overweight plus I had these issues and I could remember Guy 3 saying to me "Well, because of you and all of your issues, the baby has a hole in his heart." He blamed me. How could he do that? Why would he do that? I can remember sitting in the doctor's office, listening to him try to get me in the mood for sex, but sex was not a concern of mine. I definitely wasn't thinking about having sex with him and he knew it. Guy 3 boldly opened his mouth and said to me, "You know I hate I got you pregnant?" "I wish I would have never gotten you pregnant." Our feelings were mutual, but he offended me. There I was carrying his child, dealing with sickness in my body due to the pregnancy and this is what he said to me? "Excuse me?" I slapped him so hard, I hurt my own hand. "How dare you say that to me? You're selfish." "You're going to speak to me like this because I don't want to have sex with you?" Wow. This was Guy 3. We left the doctor that day and he was furious. He said, "You don't put your hands on me." I was wrong, but it felt right. He had been beating on me in a much worse way throughout this entire relationship. The emotional and verbal abuse he took me through cut far deeper than a slap or any punch. This was the first of three times that I had put my hands on him. My pregnancy should have been full of great memories. I should have been happy and full of joy, but I wasn't, I was miserable. This was a hard season in my life. I was pregnant by someone that I knew I had no future with. I wasn't in love with him and he certainly didn't love me. He was trying to kill the very essence of me and I was slowly dying. If you think I'm repeating myself, you're right. I am! I need you to get this and not miss a word.

I was looking forward to the purpose that was in my womb. Nehemiah would be here really soon. I tried to make things work with Guy 3, but they wouldn't. He despised the best part of me which was the God in me. God had given me a gift in my mouth, the ability to speak. He gave me the ability to interpret and internalize the word of God for myself and he hated it. He wanted a young, easy to control, senseless woman. Guy 3 hated that I was strong, young, powerful, anointed, and somewhat prepared for him woman. In other words, as many bad decisions that I've made concerning him, he knew that I wasn't just a walk in the park, but I was more of a woman than he would have liked for me to be. "Girl, you better learn how to respect your elders," is what he would say whenever I challenged what he was saying, planning, or expected. "Just humble yourself Trenee, shut up and submit." The bible says "Wives submit yourselves to your husbands," but he was not my husband and gave me no reason to even desire to want to trust him as my head.

So much wrong went on throughout the relationship, but more specifically throughout the pregnancy. It was almost time for

Nehemiah to come. My health conditions were worse and now the protein spilling into my urine was dangerous. There was a chance that I could have had seizures and my kidneys were being affected negatively. I was taken out of work and hospitalized for a few days for monitoring purposes. Shortly after, I was released and had to see a doctor once a week. My moving around was restricted.

It was on a Friday, July 6th when the doctor said to me "We have to take the baby, you're still leaking protein." That Friday, I was admitted into the hospital to be prepared for the delivery of my son. With a few hours to go until it was time; I laid there thinking about how I was 23 years old and about to be a mother. I still needed my mother greatly. How was I going to take care of this child? I found comfort in remembering a prophecy that was given to me by one of my pastors earlier that year. The prophecy was one of comfort and assurance. "Worry no more, this child will be taken care of thus saith the Lord. Don't worry about how you're going to do it. Every need will be met." Again, 23 years old, I was extremely unprepared, unmarried, and unsure about what the father would be or do, but I remembered this word.

It's time now; they were going to get my baby. I didn't get an epidural due to some difficulties with the needle and my back. I had to go under general anesthesia for the process to begin. I had to be put to sleep. 5, 4, 3, 2, 1 see you when you wake up.

Chapter 6

<u>Nehemiah is Here</u>

Trying to wake completely up, out of the best sleep I've ever had; I could hear the nurses talking while they were cleaning me up. "Congratulations! You have a beautiful baby!" I was trying to open my eyes to look around the room, but my vision was still a little blurred from the anesthesia. I was a mother! Nehemiah was no longer in me, but I was about to see him and hold him in my arms. I arrived to the room and there waited my mom and some other family members. "Tre, he's beautiful" my mom and sister said. I was in so much pain. With tears rolling down my face from both; the pain and the sight of my newborn son being rolled into the room, they gave him to me.

They were all right! He was beautiful! He was perfect! Every worry I had concerning him while I was carrying him inside me was no longer a worry. He was here and he was perfect! Nehemiah's life is the best thing that came from Guy 3. My son! I held him so tight, so close and in my heart I vowed to be the best for him. I wanted to protect him, love him, and train him to be a decent human being. I was enjoying the company and my newborn, but in my mind I was overwhelmed. I can remember thinking he's going to love me no matter what. Nothing will be able to take that away from me. From this day forth it's me and Nehemiah against the world.

I was so amazed at how my body was his home for several months. I thought about all the chaos that was going on in my body while it was sheltering him and my heart became grateful again. So much could have gone wrong, but God kept us both. I was so extremely grateful! When the people left and I was there alone with my son, I would sing to him "This little light of mine."
I would hold him close, look into his eyes and sing "There's a light in you and you got to let your light shine, Jesus is that light and you got to let your light shine. Let your light shine, let your light shine, let your light shine." Nehemiah would just look at me. I can recall talking to him and crying when we were alone in the hospital. I recall saying "I promise; Mommy will protect you from everything that I can." "I'm going to take care of you." "I love you." These moments were precious and priceless. I can also remember crying while holding him and it feeling like he knew exactly where I was and what I needed. His innocent eyes MADE me pray "God,

help me, I don't want my baby feeling what's going on in me and through me. He's too young and innocent to be exposed to this type of stuff." This is what I was saying to God, but my son comforted me. His being there made me want to be better. He made me want to toughen up and be stronger for him. He comforted me! Let me inform you. Nehemiah's name is biblical and it means "The Lord comforts." Wow! Wow because that's what Nehemiah brings into any room with him even now, the feeling of comfort. He has from the very beginning.

Anyway, the days went on and I was still in the hospital. It was now day 3 and I was ready to go, but I couldn't. I had developed a temperature and they didn't know why, so I had to stay for a week. I did not like this at all.

Guy 3 was decent during this time though. He was there every night with me and Nehemiah. He slept on a pull out chair right next to me. I thought maybe Nehemiah's birth created a real connection, that fixed every wrong thing between us; but I was wrong.

One late night while I was there in my bed and he on that pull out; Guy 3 said "Trenee, when you get out of here I need you to marry me." "If we're not going to get married, I'm done." "If you're not going to marry me, I don't want anything to do with you." He said, "I'll drop money off for the kid, but that's it." I laid there for a minute on mute. I didn't stay quiet too long though. I asked Guy 3, "Just like that, because I won't move on terms?" "What about

Nehemiah?" "I will marry you, but first we have to go through counseling with my pastors." "If we make it through the sessions, I will marry you." "I just need some things to be worked out between us first, but I'll marry you after we get and apply the help." Guy 3 said "I don't have the time for that." "I'm not going through any counseling, especially not with your pastors." "I want to marry you now." Trying to convince him, I said "We need help." "We must change some things first." I'm not going to enter into a marriage with the disagreements and differences that we have." "I can't." Guy 3 said "then I'm done" and I replied in silence with my tears. He went to sleep and I laid there thinking about the days ahead of me. He continued to be there at the hospital until I was released. He signed the birth certificate and acted as if we never had such a conversation.

The time had come! It was time to take my son home and home is where we went. Guy 3 was still there, he was acting a fool, but he was there. I can remember getting home with nothing setup downstairs and I had to put Nehemiah down; so I laid a receiving blanket on the couch in the living room and laid Nehemiah on top of it with pillows surrounding him for security. Guy 3 was out picking up some pizza and I was there talking to a next door neighbor who had come to see the new baby. He walked into the house and came into the living room where we were and started yelling "What is wrong with you? Are you crazy? Why do you have my son on this dirty furniture?" He did this right in front of company. This was embarrassing. The lady just looked at me. I took him in the kitchen and said a few things to him. I can't remember what I said, but whatever it was, he left angry. He threw the pizza in the garbage and slammed the door. This was the beginning of the ending that was really here. Slowly, but surely he started to distance himself. I remember how he started to look at me. There was literally hate in his eyes towards me.

We had a few altercations over Nehemiah during this time. I can recall one night where Nehemiah needed to be fed so I asked him "Can you feed the baby?" We were not together at this point, but we were civilized towards one another. The fact that I wouldn't marry him came up and he became upset. He put Nehemiah back in his bassinet and placed the bottle down. He tried to storm out, but I told him "You don't get to do this tonight. I don't want anything from you, but the baby didn't do anything and he still needs to be fed. "After you feed him you can leave, but tonight you are going to feed your son." I then forced Nehemiah back into his arms. I said; "Walk out on him and you'll regret it." I stood in front of the door and I wouldn't allow him to put Nehemiah down. I was angry now. This had become his pattern. He liked walking out because things weren't going his way. Guy 3 stayed and fed Nehemiah with anger in his heart towards me and my sister at this point. My sister came downstairs; tired of how he had been treating me, so she got involved. Their arguing lasted briefly. As Guy 3 sat there holding the baby, my mother placed her key in the lock and turned it. The door opened and in she walked into Drama Town, NJ. Guy 3 stood up and said "Ms. Douglas umm something went down a little while ago where I was trying to leave and Trenee shoved the baby against me and said "Feed your son." He lied and told my mom that I had hit him, which upset me even more, but it was what he said next that caused me to snap. He said "Ms. Douglas, with respect I don't want to have nothing to do with Trenee." I don't want to be in this baby's life, I just want to drop money off." This messed me up. He went from saying little stupid stuff like this to me to saying it to my mother. I lost it. I charged towards him and shoved him into a wall. "You're going to lie on me and then boldly tell somebody, you're not going to be in my child's life? Now I put my hands on you" is what I yelled to him. Again, I WAS WRONG for this, but it felt so right. My mom was blown away. "Trenee!" she yelled. "Why would you do that?" I helped him up and said "I'm sorry get up Guy 3," He said. "I'm done." "You almost broke my back" and he left. You know I chased behind him right? (Laughing out loud) I really didn't want us to end like this, but mostly because I was afraid he was going to tell the cops. (Smiling) I never did catch up with him. IT WAS OVER. Now it's just me and Nehemiah. No daddy, no husband, just mommy and son. We lived at home with my mom and sister and they helped out greatly. We were truly blessed with them being there, but again, it was not the plan to be a single mother. I was supposed to be married!

While the days ahead got harder, we continued to survive with our needs being met. God really kept his word. Every need was met and for the first year or so, I didn't buy a piece of clothing or shoes. The clothes that were given to us at the baby shower got him through his first summer. The rest of the year, my sister bought what he needed as far as clothing. We were blessed for real. My spiritual parents would sow into our lives with shoes and clothing that their children wore. We were kept! Our needs were met!

Guy 3 started back visiting for brief moments because I wanted him to be a father for real. I didn't want my son to be fatherless so I pretty much made ways for him to come. I would tell him he didn't have to deal with me, but that he needed to spend time with his son. He would come over and I would go into another room. I tried to go into another room at least, but Nehemiah wanted to be with his mommy (smiling). There was a time when he was at the house and the baby didn't have any food in the cabinets and I had no money. I showed him the empty cabinets asking him to buy the baby some food and Guy 3 replied by saying, "I don't have it." This was a lie because Guy 3 kept money. His mind was made up though. He looked at me and said "Your family won't let the baby go without food. He'll be ok."

These visits stopped and again he was gone. Guy 3 started a system where he gave money and maintained giving it for a little while. His intent was to humiliate me. Everything he gave, he made me sign a homemade receipt and if I didn't sign it, he wouldn't give me money for the baby. Nehemiah was maybe 3 months old, when these visits started. I would have loved to be in a situation that I didn't need anyone to help me take care of him, but I wasn't I needed help and again God sent the help through people. Nehemiah had so much love around him. Everybody was there. My family showed up in love for him.

One day, Guy 3 really got to me. He really got under my skin. He was so good at deceiving people. He was one way one second, but the next he was the complete opposite. He was very vindictive when it came to me. The time had come for him to give me some money. So I had a friend drive me over to his house and we waited for him outside in the car. Guy 3 came out all happy with this devilish look on his face and approached me. He said "What's up? Hey listen when are you going to let me get the kid?" I told him Nehemiah was too young and that he couldn't have him by himself without me being there. I had concerns. Well, he didn't like that. He started talking all this nonsense about what he gives and how I can take him to court and how he has receipts and so on and so forth. He continued to talk about his money and how I needed to sign the receipts and how he needs to keep them. Guy 3 said, "IF IT

WASN'T FOR ME, YOU WOULDN'T HAVE HIM." "I GOT YOU PREGNANT." I don't think I need to tell you what happened next. He handed me his receipt book laughing. After he gave me the money, I ripped the entire book up and threw it in his face. I was so extremely tired of him abusing me emotionally, mentally, and verbally. I realized that I had developed hatred in my heart for this man and it needed to be dealt with.

Picking up the pieces of ripped up paper off of the cement; Guy 3 said, "You've messed with the wrong guy, watch! You hear? You've messed with the wrong guy." "You and your family messed with the wrong one." Guy 3 must have forgotten that he told me in his younger years that he used to play with witchcraft. So as the threat left his mouth that's what I remembered in my spirit. Even though he never said these exact words; I could feel where he was going with this threat. I remained true to who I was and I stood firmly on my faith at that point and I said to him "Satan I am not afraid of you or any witchcraft." I rebuke you in the name of Jesus." He looked at me like I was crazy. He tried to rebuke some things himself, but I told him "Satan can't cast out Satan." Things were pretty complicated between us. Guy 3 continued for a brief period of time to give money, but he gave it in money orders after that incident.

I can go on and on about how Guy 3 went out of his way to make my life a living hell. Nehemiah was one now and Guy 3 had completely stopped supporting him financially. I would reach out to him needing his help with providing for "our" son and he would respond in a nasty manner. I got tired of fighting with him. So I decided to take him to court. One day out of anger; I told him, "I'm taking you to court for child support." I told him this on a few occasions. Rightfully, I should have, but it was foolish of me to disclose that information; especially out of anger. Guy 3 used the knowledge that I gave him OUT OF ANGER to prepare for the day that would come.

Court day was here. As we waited to be called up, I sat there very nervous and intimidated because he had some high class looking Caucasian attorney and I sat there alone to represent myself. To make this particular story a little shorter, Guy 3 and I had to go before a real judge because of our disagreements in front of the hearing officer. I can recall his lawyer saying "Sit right here and don't say a word, everything you want, we are going to leave with it." "I'll be right back."

We got in the court room and the show began. Guy 3 played the victim. He told the judge that he and his lawyer were afraid for his life and that from the very beginning; all I ever did was beat on him. He told the judge my mother and sister abused him. He also said he was afraid to come in the area where I lived because I was going to have someone hurt him. He lied and said I kept him from his son. As I tried to defend myself and my family, I was ordered to shut up. I was humiliated and upset. I tried to express my concern for my son being alone in the beginning with Guy 3, but again I was ordered to shut up. We left there with Guy 3 paying $70 a week and him getting visitation rights every other Sunday immediately. I had no phone number, no address and I knew nothing about where my son was going with him. Understanding biologically, yes he is the father, but a year had passed and my son really had no experience with being with him alone. I was concerned, but I had no choice; I had to yield to the court order.

Today, Guy 3 and I are cordial. We interact at Nehemiah's visiting days very briefly for the most part. He has his moments when he's a greater challenge than at other times. Because of my entire experience with him, I constantly need God to deal with me and my heart because every now and then my heart rages with hatred towards Guy 3. I need God in order for me to love him because he has wounded me inwardly. Truthfully, it's hard to totally forgive an offense when the offender constantly reminds you of what he used to do because he still tries to do the same stuff, but in a different way. My focus and energy had to shift though. It was me and Nehemiah. Whether or not Guy 3 was going to be there all the time or not, he was my son from my womb. I was going to be there and Nehemiah was definitely going to be there. It was JUST THE TWO US.

Chapter 7

<u>Just the Two of Us</u>

Wow! A whole year had passed. Nehemiah's first year went by fairly quickly. I always enjoyed my son, but now since the constant fight with his father was somewhat over, I really looked forward to enjoying him more. It was final! There was no going back trying to make anything workout for the three of us.

I watched my son grow from being carried to he himself crawling to attempting to take steps to finally walking and talking on his own. I watched him grow from being cute and innocent to cute and daring! I recall his transitions from eating baby food to eating table food. I remember him transitioning from holding his bottle to drinking out of a cup. I can remember spoon feeding him, but I also remember him fighting with me for the spoon because he wanted to feed himself.

I loved him more and more by the day. Everybody did! Nehemiah was special to me. He should have been I guess, (smiling) but he is very peculiar, is what I really mean.

There's something about his smile! Something about how he says what he says and does what he does. Anybody who knows Nehemiah knows that he'll cheer you right up. In my hardest moments of struggling as a single mom, Nehemiah's need for my parenting, love, and constant embrace kept me moving. He would look into my eyes and wrap his arms around me and say, "I love you mommy." I would smile with a full heart and say, "I love you too Nehemiah." In return, he would say "Mommy, I love you better." He would always say cute little things like this that tickled my very heart.

My little cousin, who is his big cousin, would say things like this to him and in turn he would use it when he saw fit. I was too pleased with my son. His love was pure. It was real and it was consistent. I can remember thinking it doesn't matter how imperfect I am, Nehemiah will always love me. Yeah, an everlasting love, because I am his mother! I loved the thought of this because I yearned for everlasting love. The days went on and I had so many plans for him. Most of which, I was very inconsistent with, but my heart still remains the same. I was going to always protect him. You see, Nehemiah is my miracle child. According to the doctors, remember, he's not supposed to be here. However, that was a man's report. God saw different and he gave me Nehemiah. He was shelled and carried on the inside of my chaotic womb, but came out untouched. Excuse me, but I must praise God for just a second. HALLELULAH GOD!!! His grace kept us both safe. Nehemiah was about a year and a half when I realized that I wanted to start dating again. I had been saying since his father and I decided to no longer be involved, that the next man I became involved with wasn't just going to be anybody, but he had to be someone that I believed I could build a life with. I wasn't just going to bring anyone around my son and I wasn't just going to give myself to just another guy. The next guy had to be different and I had to get the permission of God. He had to be good for my son first as well as for me. Guy 4 he was and is my gift. HE IS THAT GUY!

Chapter 8

Just Friends

It was between October and November of 2007 when we first met. I had just returned back to work from maternity leave. There had been some new hires that started while I was out. Guy 4 was one of them. A caramel toned, nicely built, bald headed, black man. I can remember seeing him for the first time. I didn't see that his head was bald in the beginning because he always wore a wave cap. I soon found out though. This was great news for me because I liked bald men. I would see him and think to myself, that he was very good to the eyes because he was extremely nice looking. Guy 4 had something going on for him that really stood out to me. I didn't even know him, but he appeared to be so very different from the guys that I'd encountered. We simply would say hello when we saw one another. I can remember talking to some female co-workers about how I found him attractive, but that was it. I never approached him.

Then one day an older co-worker came into the ladies room and said "Trenee, someone has a crush on you and thinks you're very pretty." I asked, "Who?" and she said his name. That was all I needed to know to go. I started my fishing. We became cool. We would talk when we saw each other. We worked two different shifts in two different departments, but we managed to still see each other though. (Smiling)

He would come to the department to see me and I would conveniently have to make use of the ladies room around his punch out time if I saw he hadn't come into the department by a certain time. We would talk about Christianity often. He had questions and I tried to have answers. We would just talk as friends, but I believe there was always a connection between us. However, I never thought that Guy 4 and I would ever be anything more than good friends, but my thoughts eventually didn't matter.

I can remember inviting my friend Guy 4 to a New Year's Eve service and he accepted. I was really excited that we were going to church together, but he somewhat changed the plans. I received a phone call from him maybe around 6:00p.m. Guy 4 said "Change of plans; instead of you picking me up, I'm going to meet you there because my girlfriend is coming over to Paterson." In my mind, I was like "WHAT?" I was so disappointed. I don't know if I had forgot that he had someone or not, but I was very disappointed. Oh well, there was nothing I could do about it. I went to service expecting what God was going to do in the atmosphere. They showed up and man, did he look good! I can remember thinking he resembled nephew Tommy from The Steve Harvey show that night. Bald head was shining, face was clean, and oh yea his girlfriend was pretty too. (Smiling)

Guy 4 and I continued to be friends, but I respected that he had a woman. I consistently paid attention to him though and his relationship status. I never verbally told him that I was into him, but I dropped signs often (smiling). He would talk to me as a friend concerning his relationship. We talked about things that troubled him concerning his relationship. He wanted real advice from a woman's perspective. Why not me? I showed myself to be a respectable, honest woman. (Smiling) I would give it to him too. It was real advice, untainted, and impartial. It didn't help me, but AS HIS FRIEND I really wanted to HELP HIM. So I gave him the truth. While at the same time telling him that he needed to be careful because going to the wrong woman about his relationship could be a bad thing and is inviting in a way.(If your motive is right - men, never tell another woman, your issues in your relationship concerning your woman. It only gives the unmindful woman or the woman who doesn't really care and wants you anyway an open door.)

He gave me the opportunity to cause havoc in his relationship, but I stayed appropriate and true to whom I was. I was real and respectful to even his woman, but he knew. I can recall Guy 4 would ask; "How's your son?" and I would answer, "He's good, thank you!" "How's your girl?" His answer would always be, "She's good." He was a gentlemen and I was a young woman. We never crossed boundaries; we were JUST FRIENDS.

Chapter 9

<u>From Friends to Family</u>

Our friendship lasted for about a year and a half to two and then it happened. He started to come to my department more. We even started talking on the phone a little more. One particular day was different from the rest; Guy 4 walked into my station and just stood there. Eventually he said, "Good Morning how's your day so far?" The atmosphere was very weird to me. We briefly talked and then he said "Ok, have a good day" and left. A few minutes passed and he came back and said "Trenee, I'm going to call you later." I waited for that call, but for some reason it never came.

A few weeks passed now and it was April 10, 2009 and I was at Battle Cry with the youth ministry of my church. I received a phone call and it was Guy 4. We talked a few hours that day and that was the beginning of us. I can remember asking him "How's your girlfriend?" and his response was "We are no longer together; we haven't been for a month now." I can remember getting excited inside because here was our chance. Where would it take us? I didn't know, but I wanted to find out. I wasn't waiting for my right opportunity.

It just showed up! He and I began to hang out hard at his house and also mine. It was too easy because we were already friends. I knew how I already had a strong interest in Guy 4, but now seeing him on a more personal level, intensified things for me. I had to keep in mind my vow to myself. The vow that said, the next guy I get involved with I was going to believe he was really the one and the promise to protect Nehemiah from no good men was still AT LARGE on the agenda. I had to be honest and up front about whom I was on a deeper level and what I wanted now and in the future. I laid it all on the table. I told him I wasn't looking to date him for fun, but I had every intention to get to the altar one day. I wanted to date him with a purpose. I made it clear that I needed him to totally embrace Nehemiah and I told him the kind of man I needed and I wanted him to be. He knew about how I had been hurt and let down.

One day he asked me this question; "How did you get so deeply involved with God?" "What happened?" There I was, heart beating faster and my stomach doing flips, I had to be real with him; I had to tell him the truth. I had been looking for a way to tell him this, but the time was now here. "What made me get so deeply involved with God" I repeated the question and then answered it. I explained to him my relationship with Guy 2 and how he left me with a disease to live with for the rest of my life and how God rescued me from myself and the pain that I had to face in that season of my life. That was the last thing Guy 4 expected to hear me say. There was a look of shock on his face. He even looked discouraged about me, but when I asked him was he going to walk away from what we had started, he said "No." I don't believe Guy 4 knew why for himself he didn't just walk away, but he didn't. He said that everybody deserves a chance.

That's what I love about him, his heart. He didn't reject me after hearing such hard news. Guy 4 educated himself on the disease. He asked me questions; he had a lot and I had no problem answering them. We tried to take some precaution; not as much as we could have, but we tried. He deserved the truth and the knowledge. Guy 4 didn't go anywhere, but our making it has not come easy. Remember, Guy 4 had just gotten out of a relationship. I had fallen in love with him by July. He was more than a good guy to me, he was a great guy. He helped me tremendously with Nehemiah financially. He didn't mind making sure I had what I needed if I couldn't get it. He embraced all of me.

He was a young 23 year old trying to find his place in life. He was trying to discover his purpose, define who he was as a man, get over his first real relationship and simply enjoy being young. Being in a relationship such as this one, at this point in his life wasn't easy at all. Maybe he needed time. Maybe he should have walked away, but he didn't. He decided to stay because he knew there was something different about me and this opportunity I believe. The same way I came straight and real, so did Guy 4. He told me he wanted what I wanted, but he wanted to grow to that point and that it would take time. Guy 4 told me that he just got out of a serious relationship and wasn't really looking for anything so serious right away, but I reiterated what I needed and wanted. Guy 4 boldly reiterated that he wanted to get there one day. For whatever reason, I didn't walk away either. I believe our reasons were the same or at least similar. I realized there was something different about him and this opportunity also.

I identified his value and his potential. I had embraced him and at this point, I didn't want to let him go. I believe Guy 4 had done the same for me. He has recognized my inner value, embraced it and he hasn't walked away from us yet. Again, it has been REALLY hard. For almost the first year of our relationship I was in love with him, but he wasn't in love with me. I would say, "I love you Guy 4," and he would reply by saying "Thank You, Thank You" or he would say "I'm sorry I'm not in love with you yet, but if you just give us some time I'm sure I will be." "I know I'm going to love you like that." I'm telling you, these were hard times.

I can remember waking up by the days thinking I'm in love with someone who doesn't love me back in the same way, IT WAS HARD. Everything he did said he loved me, but his mouth didn't. He had doubts about wanting to be a stepfather because he had a very bad experience as being a step child. Guy 4 struggled with totally trusting me because of past hurts from the people who said they loved him and cared. It hasn't been easy for either of us. Patience has been the key in this relationship. Guy 4 is very strong willed and so am I, so we clashed a lot. It took some adjusting; it takes some caring about each other's wants and needs. It takes us noticing what each other like and dislike. It takes us learning consistently of each other and loving one another enough to continue to grow and become better for us as a unit.

I love Guy 4 so much. He's everything I thought I didn't want, but in fact everything that I found I needed and really do want. I thought my husband would be something similar to my pastors. I thought if I didn't find him or better yet; if he didn't find me already sold out for God that he was definitely not the one. I wanted and imagined him to be everything that a Christian man looked like, but Guy 4 wasn't. He was this natural, straight forward, somewhat ghetto, swagger having, non-religious, and many questions having mature young man. He wanted God, but couldn't understand a lot of the biblical God, the true and living God ways. He wanted to discover his purpose, but couldn't see the difference between religion and relationship when it came to God. Guy 4 knew the word, he knew how to pray and all that, but he struggled with some of the principles like many of us.

A lot of our disagreements and arguments came in here. I needed him to seek God for a personal relationship and he kept calling it religion. I trust that when Guy 4 gets his personal relationship with God in order, believing his principles and ways would come a little easier. He tried for me without a real desire for the personal relationship to go to church. He would give me his word that he would make services and he did, but it was hard all by itself for him to continue to go because it wasn't for himself. I had this crazy insane plan of leaving where I was in my faith to go where he was and we'd walk back together. I bet you know it wasn't that easy. We both were stuck.

We were living a life of sex before marriage and just doing the best that we could do to be decent people, but God was definitely still unpleased. Every time I went to church the Spirit of God through the songs, through the atmosphere, through the word, convicted me. I would leave with my mind changed to do better, but find myself right back in the same place after a few weeks.

I was torn between who I was in God and who I was and liked being in the natural. Our struggle together is sex. We've battled with this for our entire relationship. Guy 4 respected my decision to wait, but I found in the beginning of us, that the error lied in me greatly. Every time that he supported me and we stopped, I went back. I continued to go to church and struggled in myself with the convictions from the Holy Spirit and my wants and fears. Fear paralyzed me. Fears of losing Guy 4 because I wanted to stay rooted in God. I was back and forth between the natural and spiritual me and I was miserable. I liked having a life outside of God, it's what I needed. I was in trouble because balance had been missing in my life. Things that should have been of a priority also, weren't. I neglected family and personal time and ignored the part of me that had never been fully dealt with in the past. My need to be loved and my low self-esteem should have been addressed. I stopped attending church for a while and I enjoyed my family; my biological family, and my family that I was trying to build with Guy 4. I was painting the wrong picture for unsaved loved ones and friends alike though. The picture was bad; but I had to get through this season of my life by making these mistakes. I believed that God was still with me. I continued to pray when I could and tried to get the word of God in me from old sermons, but for the most part I had to stay away from The House of Purpose. I could no longer handle being torn between the two because I wanted what I wanted. Eventually this season of not going to church and doing things any kind of way had to end. Guy 4 and I had to try to do things God's way. We had to try. That's what we did, we started trying together. We attended church together on Sundays. We still have ways to go and areas to grow in; but we're putting forth effort. Guy 4 has grown to embrace having a young boy child to be an example before and he is madly in love with me and me with him. (Smiling)

Guy 4 has formed a few connections with the men from my church on a very basic level. He has met with one of my pastors on a one on one basis once and I believe God for our total complete breakthrough in him. I believe that we will consistently dwell in his perfect will for our lives. We still fight against the giant of fornication daily. A lot of times, falling down, but we live to try again.

If I made my decision based on the people in the churches opinion or solely on the written words of God, I would have missed all that Guy 4 had to give me. Guy 4 came with the healing that I needed and looked for all my life. THE HEALING OF MY HEART CAME THROUGH HIM LOVING ME RIGHT. The bible says, "That man ought not to live by bread alone, but by every word that proceeds out of the mouth of God." Well, I fasted and prayed unto God concerning Guy 4 and God gave me a promise. I prayed "God, I need you to, if he's good for me, place your stamp of approval on us." At the end of the fast, the morning of the last day, I had a dream and in that dream there we were side by side with a bright light in front of us and we were walking in the direction of the light and a voice began to speak to me saying "As long as you two do things my way I will cause your relationship to last and I will surround you, but if you neglect to do right by me, I will destroy it" and we let go hands, drifted away from each other and the light.

This was God's answer to me, He was telling me that he approved and gave me instructions. Sad to say, as I already stated, we messed up, but God's grace has been sufficient. Then God spoke again Jeremiah 18:7, 8 (please read). Paraphrasing, the text basically says that if the nation that's promised destruction would turn from its sin, God promises to relent on the promised disaster. So again, Guy 4 and I do not have it all together, but I truly believe God see's our effort and knows our heart.

Guy 4 and I together have plans of a future with Nehemiah as our child with prayerfully more to come. Please know and understand that Nehemiah knows his biological father and has a relationship with him. My mother never stole that from me and Guy 4 and I will not steal that from him! As a matter of fact, Guy 3 and I finally have a decent relationship concerning Nehemiah.

It's never been easy for us, but we feel that we are worth it; so we continue to work at life individually and together. Guy 4 is the one! After 3 bad heart breaks, Guy 4 came into my life and wrapped me up in his love and IT COVERED ME.

Chapter 10

<u>Made It! Making It! Praying I'll Make It!</u>

Flashing back to one day in my work station, I was overwhelmed with my emotions and consumed by my fears. I needed to get out what I was experiencing on the inside. I didn't know exactly what it was that was turning on the inside of me, but as I begin to write; this is what came out:

Breathing deep breaths, exhaling to the fullest extent, finally I'm happy! I'm in love and he's in love with me. Everything is there, everything I ever wanted in a man is there except one thing; the will of God, which is the way of God. Before our connecting I was in God's will the best way I knew how, but I wasn't totally happy. Something was missing. Now, I have a slightly changed perspective on life and what I want and now I realize that my personal happiness and desire weighs heavy on me when they are left unattended. I now realize that love, family, laughter and family time was lacking in my world and that I was living not a lie, but not totally the truth.

Balance, discipline, wisdom, boundaries, and limitations must be implemented in my life in order for me to be totally happy and to experience joy at its fullness. I am now happier than I've ever been in my life. However, SOMEONE/SOMETHING is still missing. In the past it was "love" but now it's "LOVE," HE HIMSELF. I am in the fight of my life, needing and wanting these two different forms of love; MY FAMILY AND MY GOD!

Have you ever been torn between two different things or people that matter greatly to you? I'm sure you know what it's like to be knocked over and stepped on by life over and over and over again; by different trials and tribulations that had the potential to destroy you. Anybody ever just wanted to lie down and die? Just quit? I KNOW that I'm not alone when I say that I've wondered why me? Anybody know what it's like to try to live for other people instead of yourself and God? Have you ever just tried to please the people while you yourself were totally displeased?

My point in asking these different questions is this. On my journey called life which I've traveled for about 27 years now. I've learned a lot. I've learned that in this life WE are going to experience hard times, but we CAN'T ALLOW it to destroy us. WE will go through some things that make absolutely no sense, but WE really need to consider that we may need to continue holding on because there's a blessing coming out of it. I learned to stop worrying and to simply live consciously and with the help of God righteously. I live now with no regrets because I think about every decision I make before I make it and I live with whatever the outcome of that decision is. This leaves me with peace. If it is a wrong decision, I try to learn from it. There's no room for regretting. I found that even in my bad decisions there have been blessings awaiting me. I ABSOLUTELY DO NOT CONDONE OR AGREE with a life lived any kind of way disregarding God and his statues. Please understand me; I believe that what the bible calls sin "IS SIN." What you've read in these chapters was simply a young female on a journey to become a woman made whole, making bad decisions and poor choices. I believe that I've found my way in life, is finding my way and will continue to move forward in life.

As for God, Guy 4, and myself, we are working it out and the end is yet to be told. I believe the word of God, when it says that eyes have not seen, neither have ears heard, the things that God has in store for those who love him. I say boldly and proudly, I LOVE HIM! I LOVE GOD! For that being true; I'm expecting so much more out of life. MY PAST COULD DO NOTHING WITH ME, BUT MAKE ME BETTER. I HAVE NO COMPLAINTS. LIFE IS GOOD and GOD IS SO MUCH BETTER. BE BLESSED.

A Message to the Reader

After This, NO MORE Compromising is a memoir of my past experiences in four different major relationships. You should know that the "THIS" I'm referring to is the process. This process has been a long one for me, as you just read. It's important you know that this process first started in my mind and heart, and eventually the woman I, made strides to follow.

This is not a story that ends with a perfect ending, but it's a story that ends with me striving for perfection in life and in God. This process is a daily one! After every learned lesson, after every dead end, and after every outcome from the life altering blows; where will you find yourself in it? That's the question I want to leave you with. What are you allowing this process to get out of you? How are you acting and reacting to the process called Life? No one is exempt. Life will happen, but we must continue to live and overcome and simply grow into purpose filled fulfilling people. I told you that this is my story, but it is very well yours too.

- For the young female who's reading this book who has not yet experienced the dating scene or maybe you are right now, but haven't had to experience any of my reality- PLEASE LEARN THROUGH ME. WHAT DAMAGED ME MAY DESTROY YOU. PLEASE: LEARN THROUGH ME.

- To the young male, it's my desire that you will observe the different type of men in this book and decide to be better. MAKE UP IN YOUR MIND THAT YOU WILL NOT BE LIKE THE AVERAGE MAN. Make a difference; even in a woman's life!

- Lastly, for those of us who are somebody to someone – love each other for real. Stop taking your people for granted. What you say and do can be powerful in the life of another. LOVE EACH OTHER ENOUGH TO PROTECT ONE ANOTHER- YES; FROM EVEN YOU. IT MATTERS!

AND IF YOU HAVE ANY UNFORGIVENESS IN YOUR HEART FOR ANYTHING TOWARDS ANYONE – PLEASE COME FACE TO FACE WITH IT AND LET IT GO. REMEMBER IT'S A PROCESS. FORGIVE THEM... NO LONGER MIND "IT"

THANK YOU!!!

- First, I must thank God for keeping me and holding me. He truly has never let me go. His grace has kept me from being consumed and his love continues to lift me. He is the most consistent in my life. He's thinking about me, even when I'm not thinking about him. I love Him!

- A huge special thanks to my mother, who is straight up the greatest in my eyes. She's my superhero. When all hell was breaking loose in my personal life; she was right there drying my tears, and wiping snot from my nose. She comforted me. She was even ready to go to war a few times. (smiling) Gwendolyn Renace Barbee Douglas I love you mama!

- To my sister who has also been a part of my support system at home. She drives me up a wall, but I can't imagine life without her. Thank you Nee for supporting this project with your money, time and input.

🕂 Big brother, I thank you for encouraging me always to do what I'm good at. Every chance you get, you speak kind words to me. I appreciate the love. My Favorite: "Shine because you're a star!" (I love that)

🕂 To my son Nehemiah, you are truly the greatest gift in human form that I could have ever been given. I love you!

🕂 To my gift Vaughn, thank you for believing in me, and supporting me and this writing project. Thank you for your financial contribution and the time you spent reading this book as I was writing it. You are the best!

🕂 Naomi Bruce, thank you for believing enough in this book, that you sowed into it. God bless you!

🕂 To my spiritual parents, Pastors Derrick & Darrell Etienne and Ladies Shamone & Zalika Etienne I love all four of you so very much! Thank you for teaching me about purpose and destiny. Thank you for being key people in my life and thank you for loving me with the love of God no matter what. I know that as your spiritual daughter, I've had my ups and downs right before you. There were moments when I fell and you were there. Times when I struggled within myself and with his will and you were there. I've called myself taking breaks from the ministry to do my own thing, but still you always remained right there. Thank you for depositing someone and something into me that I will never be able to lose nor forget. The truth, GOD! And my faith. *Proverbs 22:6 * **Train up a child in the way that he should go, and when he is old, he will not depart from it.** I was nineteen when I first I got saved in your ministry. I am now twenty seven years old and as I've already stated, I've strayed off a lot, but I cannot deny whose I am and who I am. I BELONG TO GOD.

⊥ David Robinson, awesome work man! Thank you for a beautiful book cover.

⊥ Dariel Johnson, thanks big cousin for editing for me. You are a life saver!

⊥ A special thank you to those who distributed the promotional flyers. Specifically: Nef, U.Anthony, Auntie Shawn, Brittany, Nee Nee, Felicia, Julie, Juwan, Vaughn, Rafon and my nephew Kirk-Kirk. Thank you all!

⊥ Auntie Mona & Auntie Shawn, thanks for reading along in the beginning. Your feedback was definitely needed. I love you both.
Auntie Shawn, you are my biggest fan! You motivated me so much during this process.

⊞ Auntie Tre, thank you for putting me on that basketball team! I truly believe basketball kept me shielded and away from the foolishness growing up in the jects. Basketball taught me discipline, and how to submit to authority. Thank you!

⊞ Lastly, but not least, I want to thank guys 1-3! I thank you because had you not painted the clear picture of who you were and how you moved; I would not be able to recognize nor identify the kind of man that I want and need today. You enable me to know exactly the kind of man that I do not want or need in my life. THANK YOU!

www.ingramcontent.com/pod-product-compliance
Lightning Source LLC
Chambersburg PA
CBHW031250280526
45784CB00004B/1795